362.2
9.90

Homelessness

Kaye Stearman

WAYLAND

Talking Points series
Alcohol
Animal Rights
Charities – Do They Work?
Divorce
Genocide
Homelessness
Mental Illness
Slavery Today

Produced for Wayland Publishers Limited by
Discovery Books Limited, Unit 3, 37 Watling
Street, Leintwardine, Shropshire SY7 0LW,
England

Editor: Patience Coster
Series editor: Alex Woolf
Designer: Simon Borrough
Consultant: Brian Strand Milne

First published in 1998 by Wayland Publishers
Ltd, 61 Western Road, Hove, East Sussex BN3
1JD, England

Find Wayland on the internet at
http://www.wayland.co.uk

**British Library Cataloguing in Publication
Data**
Stearman, Kaye
  Homelessness. – (Talking points)
  1. Homelessness – Juvenile literature
  I. Title
  362.5

ISBN 0-7502-2178-X

Printed and bound in Italy by G. Canale
C.S.p.A., Turin

Acknowledgements
The author would like to thank the following
for their valuable assistance: Lars P Ludvigsen
(UN Centre for Human Settlements – Europe
Office), Sigrid Shayer, Anne Stearman, and
housing and settlement organizations in the
UK and elsewhere.

Picture acknowledgements
Axiom 28 (Jim Holmes); Getty Images 12
(Gerard Del Vecchio); Images of India 36 (S D
Manchekar); Impact Photos 10 (Mark
Henley), 23 (Daniel White), 30 (Jorn
Stjerneklar), 38 (Tadashi Kajiyama), 47 (Chris
Kelly), 50 (David Lurie), 52 (Peter Arkell), 53
(Daniel White), 56 and 59 (Francesco Rizzoli);
Hutchison Library 5 (Crispin Hughes), 13
(Sarah Errington), 34, 39, 49 (Lesley Nelson);
Panos Pictures 4 (Börje Tobiasson), 6 (Penny
Tweedie), 7 (Howard Davies), 8 (Philip
Wolmuth), 9 (Betty Press), 11 (Philip
Wolmuth), 14 (Alberto Arzoz), 15 (Sara Leigh
Lewis), 16 (Trygve Bølstad), 17 (Chris
Stowers), 18 (Melanie Friend), 19 (Peter
Barker), 20 (J C Tordai), 21 (Peter Barker),
24 (Paul Smith), 25 (Paul Harrison), 26 (Eric
Miller), 29 (Javed Jafferji), 31 (Peter Barker),
32 (Trygve Bølstad), 33 (Peter Fryer), 35 (Sean
Sprague), 40 (Hamish Wilson), 41 (Seamus
Murphy), 42 (Marc French), 43 and 44
(Morris Carpenter), 46 (Sean Sprague),
48 (Jim Holmes), 54 (Cedric Nunn), 55 (Ron
Giling), 57 (Neil Cooper), 58 (Sean Sprague);
WHO/UNICEF 22 (S Rotner).

Cover picture: A refugee girl living in a
drainpipe on the outskirts of Calcutta
(Format/Maggie Murray).

Contents

Talking about homelessness

What images do we summon up when we hear the word 'homeless'? Let's listen in to a group of young people discussing the subject:

'It's obvious isn't it – they're people who don't have nowhere to live – the ones you see begging in the streets. At night they sleep in doorways.'

'And some of them are crazy, or they drink a lot... no one wants them because they are too drunk and dirty.'

'Not everyone's like that – some of them have lost their jobs and they can't afford somewhere to live. And it's really difficult to get another job because you don't have any place to wash or change your clothes or anything.'

'There's a girl at our school from Somalia. She said her family came here because their home was destroyed in the war. Now they live with relatives but it's very crowded. So she's homeless twice – once in her country and once over here.'

'That's right. And there's another girl who lives in a hostel and they have to share a kitchen with five other families and they don't know each other's languages.'

'When we lived in the country, there were people who would come around and do some casual work and then go off again.... '

'But you can't call them homeless can you? I mean, they like living like that, a bit like gypsies. They could settle down if they wanted to.'

Different voices, different views, different experiences. Together they show some of the ways people might be homeless in our society. They

Talking point

'The average life expectancy of a person living rough is 47. The normal average life expectancy is 73 for a man and 78 for a woman.'

From the Crisis report, *Sick to Death of Homelessness.*

If you were made homeless tomorrow, which aspects of life on the streets do you think would most affect your health? What would you miss about life at home?

A homeless man on the streets of New York.

also show that our ideas of homelessness are shaped by where we live, what we see and who we know. But if we look beyond, to the wider world, we see that there are many different ways of living through the experience of being homeless. In the following pages we look at four stories from four countries: India, Australia, the USA and Montserrat.

Many homeless refugees build their own shelters, using whatever materials are available. These Somalians now live in a refugee camp in Kenya.

Defining homelessness

Defining homelessness is very difficult but, broadly speaking, it can be divided into the following categories:
• rooflessness (people sleeping rough)
• houselessness (people in shelters, institutions or short-term accommodation)
• insecure housing (people in squats or refugee camps)
• inadequate or inferior housing (people in houses without basic facilities)
In practice, it is not always possible to separate the different categories, especially as housing standards vary from country to country.

Maya's story

Maya lives on the pavements of Bombay, India's largest city, in a tiny hut made from pieces of tin and plastic sheets. Her family eat, sleep, dress and store their few possessions inside the hut while Maya cooks outside on the pavement. There is no running water or electricity and the roof leaks in the monsoon rains. Maya has never had electricity or water or a strong roof or privacy, so she can cope without these things: her main worry is insecurity.

Maya and her family live in a makeshift shelter on the pavement in Bombay.

Maya worries that her husband will be injured at work or that there will be no work, or that her children might be injured in the ceaseless traffic. She worries that the city government will demolish her hut because they want the city to look more attractive for rich residents and tourists; even if her hut is not demolished, she's concerned that it will be destroyed in a gang fight or a riot. Maya has shelter, but she has no home and no security.

This Vietnamese refugee family has just arrived in Australia. Refugees may find it difficult to adjust to a new country and a different way of life.

Trung's story

Trung, who lives in Melbourne, Australia, is also homeless. When he left home he spent several nights sleeping outside. Now he stays with friends, moving from house to house. He attends school occasionally, but will probably drop out when he turns sixteen.

Trung was born in Vietnam. Before they settled in Australia, Trung and his family spent years in a refugee camp in Malaysia. He left home at the age of fourteen, after family conflicts. Trung says his parents are too strict; they expect him to follow Vietnamese ways. He feels that he is Australian and he wants more freedom. One day his father caught him smoking a cigarette and threw him out of the house.

Trung survives homelessness because of the support of his friends – but he is unhappy and insecure. He doesn't have an income and he's too young to get social security. Without a decent education he is unlikely to find a good job, so he won't be able to earn enough to afford a proper place to live. He might turn to crime, or drift into life on the streets. Really, he'd like to go back home, but doesn't see how he can.

Lenny's story

The temperature is below zero in Milwaukee, USA, and Lenny is glad he's finally out of the cold. Tonight he's found a place in a shelter run by a charity. He gets a bed and food. There's nothing much to do there but that's okay – it's good to be off his feet. The nights are the worst. The shelter is very overcrowded and Lenny worries about his possessions – not that he's got much, but he knows that people will steal anything.

Lenny has been on the move for years. Once he could cope with anything, there was always some way of getting by – the odd job, a lucky break. But now he's not so sure. He's been run down by a car and beaten up several times, and lately he's been coughing blood. The nurse at the shelter says that it's tuberculosis and he should stop travelling and get proper treatment. Maybe he will – but he's lived like this for so long that he doesn't know whether he can change.

Winter is especially hard if you are homeless. In some countries, charity organizations run shelters offering food, warmth and safety.

Merle's story

Merle is frightened and apprehensive. Two years ago, life was good on the island of Montserrat in the Caribbean. Then, in 1995, the volcano called Chance's Peak erupted. Red-hot lava rushed down the slopes – covering the fertile land, destroying houses, roads, schools and churches. Merle's family left their farm and went to live in the northern part of Montserrat. At first they thought that this would be a temporary arrangement. They'd often slip back to harvest their crops, even though the farm was in the dangerous 'forbidden zone'.

Months went by – and there was no return. More people came to the north. There was no proper housing, so people lived in temporary shelters or large tents. Everyone was overcrowded and people felt bitter, frustrated and confused. Many people left the island: of Montserrat's 12,000 people, 8,000 left in two years. Merle's family don't know whether to go or stay. Life in the overcrowded shelters seems like no life at all; but if they leave, they will be homeless.

What connects these stories? All these people are homeless, even though they may have some form of shelter. Maya lives in a makeshift hut, Trung is in temporary accommodation, Lenny is in a shelter for the homeless and Merle is waiting for a new home. Despite their problems, Maya and Merle have the love and support of their families to sustain them. Trung would like to return to his family. Lenny left family life behind long ago.

Homelessness may be brought about by natural disasters and war. During war, people's homes are often deliberately destroyed by soldiers. This destroyed village is in southern Sudan.

Different countries have different standards. Trung sleeps on his friend's floor, but the room he uses is four times the size of Maya's pavement hut and has running water and electric light – things Maya can only dream of. Lenny lives in the USA, one of the richest countries in the world, but he suffers from tuberculosis, a disease of poor people.

Homelessness is a difficult problem to talk about because normally we only see the problems that are most visible or obvious to us. This means that it is hard to measure how many people are homeless. Do we count only the people living on the streets? What about people in temporary accommodation or in shelters? Do we consider people forced to leave their homes by war or natural disasters? What about people living in overcrowded or unsuitable accommodation – should they also be considered as homeless? Many of these questions are controversial and often there are no clear answers.

Keeping these questions in mind, we will look at some of the causes and experiences of homelessness during the course of this book. We will also consider how we might end homelessness and ensure that every person has the right to a safe place to live.

Some homeless people have no shelter at all. In countries around the world, people sleep on city pavements. This Chinese family is probably looking for work in the city.

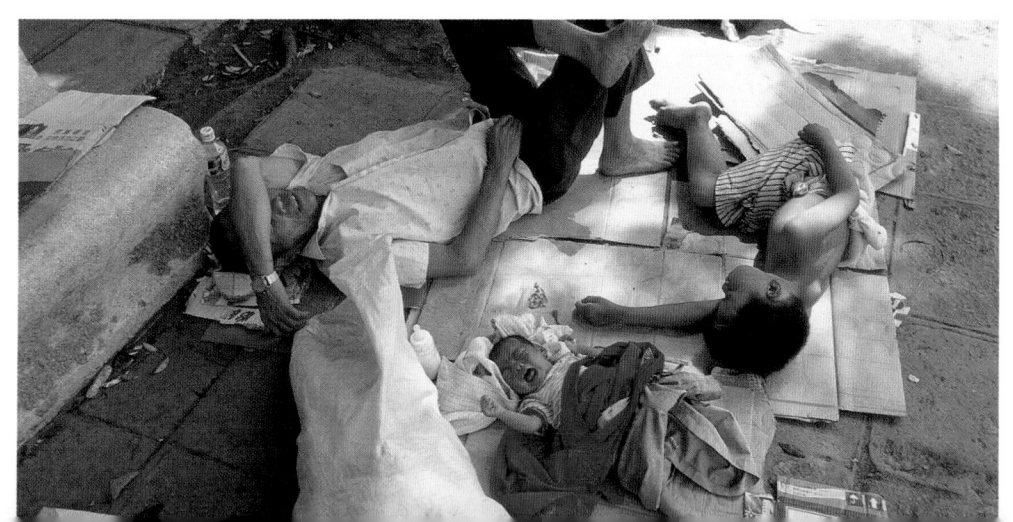

How many homeless people?

The numbers of homeless people worldwide are not known. One problem is that census figures may not be accurate. Another problem is that many people are homeless on a temporary, rather than permanent, basis. However, one estimate from the United Nations Centre for Human Settlements (Habitat) gives between 40 million and 200 million roofless and houseless people worldwide, and between 500 million and 1,500 million (one and a half billion) in insecure and inadequate housing. Most homeless people live in Asia, Africa and Latin America.

There are also homeless people in rich countries. Of the 340 million people in the European Union (15 countries), around 18 million are estimated to be homeless or badly housed, including 1.8 million who are roofless and houseless. Of the 250 million people in the USA, government figures say that 250,000 to 350,000 are roofless and houseless; a non-government organization, the National Coalition for the Homeless, puts the figure at between three million and seven million.

Refugees in western countries are often housed in overcrowded, unhealthy conditions, like this 'bed-and-breakfast' in London.

Leaving the land

Talking point

'I never thought of our land as a "wilderness". To us, it's a place to live and find food.... But white people think that... no one should be allowed inside because it's too fragile. So they put a fence around it – even though we have lived there for generations.'

Ruby Dunstan, Chief of the Nklap'mux people, British Columbia, Canada.

Is it acceptable to evict people from their land for environmental reasons?

Once most people made their living from the world around them. Even today, about half the world's population still lives in this way – growing crops, herding animals, fishing, hunting and gathering. Although life can be very hard, it can also be rewarding. During a good season, food is plentiful; there is space to move and to build. People feel that their land, their home and their way of life are worth the hardships.

Some people leave the land because they are attracted by life in the cities. However, many people leave because the land can no longer support them. Forests are felled to make way for commercial farms, or logged for timber. In densely populated countries the soil is used even more intensively, as tiny farms are divided into smaller plots. Water supplies dry up or are polluted by pesticides, factory waste or sewage. Small farmers cannot compete with large farms, which are often run by big companies.

About half the world's population still lives on the land, growing crops and tending animals, like these farmers in Morocco.

Destruction of the land

'Environmental degradation' is the term used when forests are destroyed, fertile soils are exhausted, or water supplies are polluted or dry up. One area which has seen widespread environmental degradation is the Niger River delta in south-eastern Nigeria, home of the Ogoni people. Once this area had rainforests and mangrove swamps. Most Ogoni were small farmers, carefully cultivating their land, growing yams, cassava and other vegetables and fishing from the abundant waters.

In 1956, oil was discovered in the Niger delta. Big oil companies, like Shell Oil, moved into the area. They built a huge refinery, fertilizer plant and dozens of well-heads. Oil pipelines criss-crossed the villages. Oil and waste began to seep into the water supply, poisoning the fish and poisoning the people who used it for washing and drinking. Gas flares flamed day and night, producing soot which settled on the fields, rivers and people's homes and coated people's skin and lungs.

A common sight in the **Niger delta – a rural scene with an oil refinery in the background.**

13

Ken Saro-Wiwa, a well-known author and journalist, formed the Movement for the Survival of the Ogoni People (MOSOP) to protest against the destruction of the land. Thousands of people protested against the actions of the government and Shell Oil. The government responded brutally, arresting, torturing and imprisoning the MOSOP leaders. In November 1995, Ken Saro-Wiwa and eight others were executed.

The army killed over 3,000 people and injured many thousands more. They went into the villages, drove people away, stole food, killed animals and burnt down homes. Ogoni were forced from their land and homes. For months people hid in the bush, finding food as best they could. The injured could not go to health centres or hospitals; they knew that if they came out of hiding they would be killed.

There were worldwide protests against Shell Oil, after the Nigerian government executed Ken Saro-Wiwa and eight other Ogoni activists.

About 50,000 Ogoni became refugees and displaced people (see Chapter 6). Some escaped to other countries, but most fled to other parts of Nigeria. Those who remain must live off their damaged land and

A crude oil spill in Ogoniland, where destructive oil refining has polluted the air, the land and the water.

poisoned water. Unless things change, many more will be forced to leave their homes.

The pressures to leave

Today, worldwide, many people are forced to leave their homes because other people decide that their land is valuable – whether for roads, houses, factories, farming, mining, logging, dams, tourism or other types of 'development'. These pressures are not new. In the eighteenth century, powerful Scottish landowners decided that it would be more profitable to use their land for sheep than for small-scale farming, so they destroyed the homes of the tenant farmers and drove them away. In the so-called 'highland clearances', thousands of people were made homeless. Most left for the growing industrial cities or migrated to North America or Australia.

The Scottish landowners saw themselves as enlightened people bringing progress to backward areas. Today, governments and companies often use the same arguments. They argue that roads will open up an isolated area, that a mine will bring in valuable foreign currency, that a tourist complex will create much-needed jobs. The fact that these projects make people homeless is seen as less important than the benefits they may bring. Protest against such projects is often difficult, or dangerous.

The Three Gorges Dam

In central China, a series of huge dams is under construction along the Yangtze River. The scheme – known as the Three Gorges Dam – is intended to stop the destructive flooding of the Yangtze and provide badly-needed electricity for homes and industry. When the dam is finished, 1.9 million people will have lost their homes under the waters. Half of these people are farmers, the other half live in the cities along the riverbank. Some people feel that the dam will improve their lives; many others, especially the farmers, do not want to leave.

The construction of the Three Gorges Dam in China is one of the world's largest engineering projects.

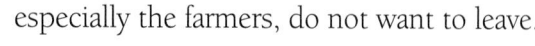

Case study

Zheng Xiaolong is a farmer. For hundreds of years his family has farmed land on the slopes above the Yangtze River. But the building of the Three Gorges Dam means that he will lose both his home and his livelihood:

'Our home is here,' says Zheng, 'our temples are here. Most importantly, the graves of our ancestors are here. Everything will be submerged under the waters. But the government has decided – what can I do?' When the time comes to move, Zheng will take everything he can, even the house timbers and the grave markers. After that the house will be destroyed so that no one will be able to return. The government says that Zheng will receive compensation and a new home, but he will have no right to bargain about the amount of money or to decide where to go. All the sites for new housing are chosen by the government.

The people from Zheng's village have been promised that they will be resettled on agricultural land. However, it is unlikely to be as good as the land they are leaving, so Zheng and the other farmers may have to find extra work. Some will probably join the 'floating people' who work on building sites and in factories in China's booming cities. Already there are over 20 million homeless 'floating people'. They join the growing numbers of homeless people in cities worldwide.

In China and many other countries around the world, homeless rural people drift to the cities in search of work.

Escaping rural poverty

During the Depression of the 1930s, millions of North Americans abandoned their land and homes. Some were poor farmers who lost their farms to drought and dust-storms. Others were black sharecroppers who left the south to escape poverty and racism. In both cases, people were victims of environmental degradation. Some of the migrants became agricultural labourers in more fertile areas, but most left the land to work in city factories.

Today, the same pattern is being repeated in other parts of the continent. Millions of poor farmers from Mexico and Central America can no longer make a living from their degraded land. Most go to the capital city, others migrate to the USA on a temporary or permanent basis.

According to the United Nations, an estimated 1 billion (1,000 million) of the world's rural people live in poverty. Of these, 52 per cent do not have enough land to support themselves and 24 per cent are landless.

Many poor Mexicans migrate to the USA to pick crops such as grapes and tomatoes. The work is hard and the pay is low, but it is better than living in poverty at home.

Shelter in the cities

Talking point

'I and my friends live just a few minutes away from this beautiful headquarters. My home is Kenya's Mathare Valley, one of Africa's largest and poorest slums. We have none of the things you have here. We lack clean water, roads, electricity, toilets, garbage collection, health care and security. A major threat to our lives is the lack of clean water. For that water we pay three to four times more than the rich people living in the elite Muthaiga area next door.... Our families are crammed into small plots and shelters, most owned by others. We live on borrowed time and borrowed land. There would be enough resources to meet everyone's needs – if we eliminated greed.'

Maurice Njoroge, speaking on behalf of the world's youth, at the Governing Council of the United Nations Environmental Programme, Nairobi, Kenya, February 1997.

Do you believe that a fairer distribution of wealth would help to solve the global problems of homelessness and poverty?

Millions of people in towns and cities all over the world know what it is like to be without a proper home. Some of these people exist in the inner city, living on the pavements, sleeping in doorways or empty buildings, or in flimsy, makeshift shelters. Others survive in sprawling shanty towns on unused and waste land. Countless others are forced to stay in decaying slums or inadequate housing, or they have to crowd in with relatives and friends while they search for a place of their own.

The Mathare Valley in Nairobi is one of Africa's largest slums. Life here is unhealthy because of the lack of clean water.

The growing cities

In the last few decades, nearly all countries have experienced a growth in their urban populations. Half the world's population now lives in urban areas, although the proportion varies in different regions (see table opposite). Many of the fastest-growing cities are in developing countries where, until recently, most people lived on the land. However, not all of the new population comes from rural migrants. Increasingly, city growth comes from the people already living there. People migrate to, or continue living in, cities because they offer opportunities to find jobs, gain an education and have fun; but finding affordable housing can be difficult.

Cairo, on the banks of the River Nile in Egypt, is one of the world's most ancient cities. Today it has a population of almost nine million. An estimated one million live in an ancient cemetery known as 'The City of the Dead'; half-a-million people occupy roof-tops and millions of others live in squatter

In crowded slums, such as this in Manila in the Philippines, children must play in the streets. There is nowhere else for them to go.

A graveyard for a playground. Children perched on the edge of the City of the Dead in Cairo, Egypt.

settlements or share crowded rooms. Few of these people would be called 'homeless', but many live in housing that is overcrowded and with few facilities.

In some cities, rich and poor people live side-by-side but increasingly they live in different, segregated areas. In western countries, better-off people often live in suburbs or commuter towns. Good transport links carry them to work in the city centres and bring them home each day. As inner city areas become run-down and crime and vandalism increase, people move away and jobs disappear. Only the poorest people remain. Once again, most of them would not be called 'homeless', even though they face an insecure future in poor housing.

People living in urban areas, 1990

Latin America/ Caribbean	71.4%
USA	82%
W. Europe	75%
China	26%
India	25%

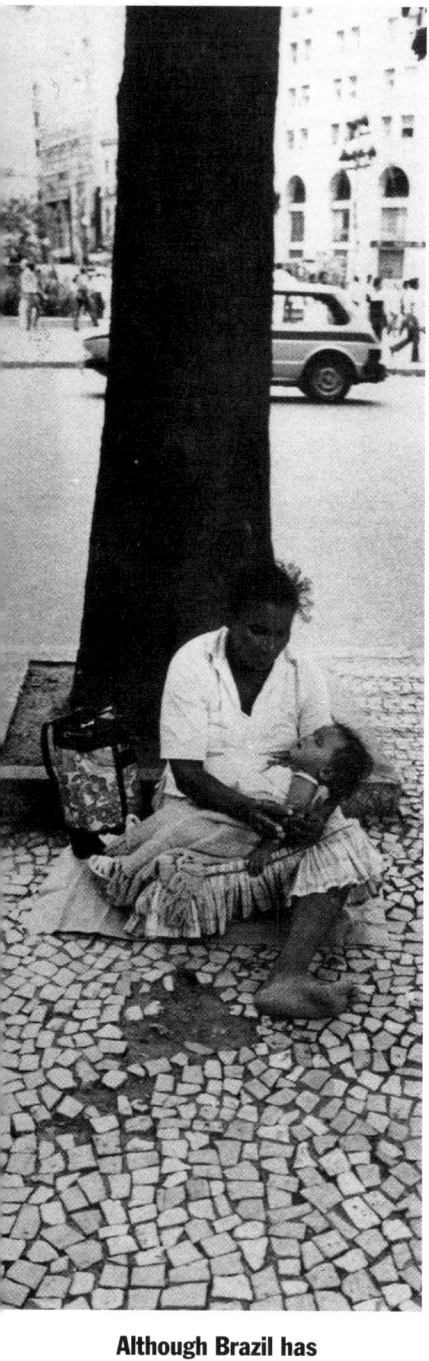

However, in many cities and towns worldwide, more and more people are truly homeless – the streets are their only home. Conditions vary in different cities and countries. The greatest numbers of homeless people are found in developing countries with the largest cities, such as India, Indonesia and Brazil, but there are homeless people in the towns and cities of developed countries, too. Some homeless people are very visible, building small shelters on the pavements of the city; others may spend their nights sleeping rough under bridges or in doorways. Some homeless people move – or are moved on – constantly from place to place; others remain in the same area for a number of years.

Pavement dwellers

Maya, who we met in Chapter 1, is one of at least 250,000 people living on the streets of Bombay. She has been there for twelve years. At first the family lived in the open, later they built their shelter. No one knows the exact numbers of pavement dwellers, as they don't appear in city censuses or on voting registers. The city authorities do not want people living on the pavements and have made many attempts to move them. But later, after the pavements have been cleared, the people come back. They have nowhere else to go.

Yet pavement dwellers make a valuable contribution to Bombay. Like Maya, nearly all work for their living, as labourers, street traders or as servants to the rich. Some could afford to pay for better housing in outlying areas but there is little work there and they could not afford the fares to travel to and from the city. And, with more people arriving each year, there would always be workers to take their place.

Although Brazil has prosperous cities, they contain many poor and homeless people who live on the streets.

The people who are most likely to be homeless are those who are poor or who lack family support. Many homeless people are born into poverty and never escape it. For example, Maya's children growing up on the pavements have little opportunity to attend school regularly. Even at an early age they have to work to contribute to the family's survival. Without education or skills, they have almost no chance of escaping poverty.

Shelters made of plastic sheets weighted down with stones are a common sight on the pavements of Bombay, India's richest city.

City squalor

The United Nations estimates that there are at least 600 million urban dwellers in Africa, Asia and Latin America who live in 'life and health threatening' homes and neighbourhoods, without clean water, sanitation, drainage or rubbish collection. Tens of millions live in shacks on the pavements or sleep in the streets or public places.

'Street children' are a common sight in Bombay. These children spend their days – and often their nights – on the streets. Like homeless adults, most street children are workers. Usually they provide some sort of service – running errands, carrying shopping, shining shoes, serving in small hotels or tea shops. Some search the streets for bottles or cardboard that can be resold for a tiny profit; some pick through piles of rubbish for items they can use or sell. Some children beg or steal, either individually or as part of a group or gang. Many sleep on the streets, not in makeshift huts like Maya's family, but wherever they can find shelter – in alleyways and shopfronts, under bridges or stairways, by railway sidings or bus stations.

There are millions of street children in the world. The majority live in Asian and Latin American cities, and there are increasing numbers in Africa, Eastern Europe and the former Soviet Union. However, there are also street children in North America, Europe and Australia. Most street children are boys.

Street children

It is often assumed that all street children are homeless, but this is not always the case. Street children can be divided into two major categories.
• Children on the street – children who work on the streets to help support their families and return home each night. They are not homeless, although they may live in poor housing. They are the largest group of street children.
• Children of the street – children who have left their families and live, work and sleep on the streets. Some join gangs or informal groups for protection and friendship.

Street children work at some of the worst-paid and most unhealthy jobs. These Indian children recycle rubbish.

Case study

Juan is one of many thousands of children on the streets of Bogota, the capital city of Colombia. Here is a snapshot of his life:

At the age of twelve, Juan has already spent three years on the street. At first he begged and looked for food in rubbish bins. He still does this occasionally but now he is much more streetwise – he knows the best places to find money, food and drugs. One reason Juan survives is because he belongs to a gang of boys and girls who look out for each other. They hang out around the same area, share food and drugs and watch for the police, whom they fear. They run errands, wash car windows and look after parked cars until the owners return. The older children protect the younger ones from bullying by other gangs; they care for members who are ill or disabled as best they can.

Juan enjoys sniffing glue, which is cheap and readily available. But sniffing numbs him to his surroundings. He was hit by a car when he was high on glue and his shoulder was broken, but he was soon back on the streets, sniffing glue again. As he gets older he may start taking harder drugs like coca paste and cocaine or he may sell his body for sex or become involved in criminal activities. Juan doesn't think too much about the future – what's the point?

Juan hasn't lost all contact with his family. They live in a *barrio* (shanty town) on the outskirts of Bogota, but it's a long way to travel so he doesn't see them too often. He has bitter memories of being beaten by his father and older brother. He never liked school much – life on the streets is freer and more exciting. Although he is homeless, he feels more at home on the streets than he did living with his family.

Juan often prefers sniffing glue to eating food. Glue makes him feel happy and helps him to forget his troubles.

Evicted!

Talking point

'We didn't want to go, but we had to. We appealed to our local councillor to help us but, when the day came, he was there with the police. Some had guns. Nobody wants to die, so we packed up our things, took what we could carry from our houses.... They brought us here – here where there is nothing.'

Jamilla, Karachi, Pakistan

'I was eleven when the bulldozers came for the first time. The government said we couldn't live there and forced us out. We have had to move many times since then. Now we are back in the city. This time we mean to stay.'

Evelyn, Cape Town, South Africa

Every year, hundreds of thousands of people lose their homes and their livelihoods through evictions. Should people be protected from eviction by private landlords and governments? If so, how?

Jamilla, from Karachi, and Evelyn, from Cape Town, are typical of many poor city dwellers. They cannot afford to buy or rent housing, so they have to provide for themselves. They find land that is not being used, or where there is still some space, and build their own homes. The land may be owned by private landlords, companies, government departments, the military (sometimes no one knows who it really belongs to); or it might be 'common land' – neither public nor private but open to everyone. As the people don't own the land they live on, they have few or no legal rights to remain there. Sometimes they pay rent to landlords or hand money over to the authorities as compensation or bribes, but this rarely gives them rights as tenants. In effect, these people are squatters.

Evictions are sudden and often brutal. Homes and possessions are destroyed and families split up.

How many evictions?

Many people who are evicted are not registered with city authorities or counted in censuses. Even though they have lived in an area for years, they are classified as squatters or as illegal residents. They are unlikely to have documents proving they own or have rights to land, housing or possessions.

One organization estimates that, in Asia, 200,000 to 300,000 families are evicted each year – a total of between one and two million people. In both the Philippines and India there are at least 200,000 people evicted each year. There are also large-scale evictions in Latin America and Africa.

In developing countries, many city dwellers live in houses and neighbourhoods that have been developed illegally. For example, in Karachi, where Jamilla lives, there are over 500 squatter settlements, known as *katchi abadis*. Four-and-a-half million people live in the *abadis* – 45 per cent of the city population. *Katchi abadis* are often located on government land near city centres. Jamilla's *katchi abadi* was one of these. The makeshift shelters erected by the residents became more permanent as time went by. Some were even made of concrete and had tiled roofs. Through their own efforts, people managed to acquire electricity, water-taps and toilets. Local politicians sought their support and promised them that the settlement would be protected.

People living in the *katchi abadis* of Karachi work hard to improve their situation.

The authorities did not object when the *abadi* was first settled. The *abadi* residents provided valuable services. The men worked in the factories, pulled carts or sorted waste. Some of them were traders or ran tea stalls. Some of the women worked as servants in the houses of rich people. However, as land prices rose, politicians and businessmen saw how much money could be made from selling the land for offices, banks and luxury housing. There was suddenly a profit to be made from getting rid of squatters and clearing the land.

Razed to the ground

Jamilla and her family knew nothing of this until a local councillor came one morning and told them that they had to go. He told them not to worry, they would get another site. The people pleaded not to be evicted. They had already spent all their spare money on building and improving their houses – how could they leave them? And where was the other site? They knew of nowhere close by. Their pleading had no effect. One week later, armed police arrived. The government bulldozers began to demolish buildings. People who tried to resist were beaten up, some were shot. In the end, the whole *katchi abadi* was razed to the ground.

The families were taken to another area. They were told that this was to be their new home and that they would have more space than before. They had more space, but everything else was much worse. The new site was miles away from the city centre and had no amenities – no electricity, no toilets – just one tap to be shared between 300 people. There were no jobs locally, so the men had to spend two hours travelling to and from their work on the bus each morning and evening. People were expected to buy their new plots of land and build new houses – all with less money than before.

In Karachi there are over five hundred squatter settlements like this, housing millions of people.

Evelyn is a black South African. She has spent most of her life moving from one temporary settlement to another. From 1948 to 1994, South Africans lived under a system called apartheid (apartness). Everyone was placed into a group according to their racial background: Whites; Bantu (all Africans); Coloureds (people of mixed ancestry) and Indians (descendants of immigrants from India). But people didn't share equally; the government said that the whites were superior and should have the best land, houses, jobs and education. Until recently, all black people in South Africa were expected to live in rural 'homelands', or in special segregated areas of the cities. People who lived in the 'wrong' areas (outside the homelands and segregated areas) risked eviction, arrest and imprisonment.

During the apartheid regime, millions of black South Africans were forced to settle in shanty towns like New Crossroads (near Cape Town).

Life under apartheid

Evelyn's family has always lived in 'wrong' areas and therefore was always being evicted. Her parents were forced off their farm when the government said it was 'white land'. They came to live in District Six, a poor, racially mixed area of Cape Town. In the 1960s, the government abolished racially mixed areas. The family then went to live in a shanty town called KTC, situated on windy sand-dunes outside Cape Town. Evelyn's family couldn't even build a proper house, but they were desperate for somewhere to live. There were so many police raids that people built shelters of plastic: they hid these in the sand during the day and rebuilt them at night. This went on for years.

Poor people living as squatters can suddenly be evicted to make way for new developments. A luxury hotel in Phnom Penh, Cambodia, is skirted by shanty dwellings – but for how long?

By the late 1980s, the apartheid system was crumbling. When a new non-racial government was elected in 1994 it was determined to end the huge injustices brought about by apartheid. Every person was granted equal rights to live, work and move freely. The old laws that restricted people's right to live where they wanted were abolished.

Olympic evictions

The building of new facilities for a major international event, such as the Olympic Games, is often given as a reason to evict poor people. When the 1988 Olympic Games were awarded to Seoul, the city evicted over 700,000 people to make way for the sports facilities and Olympic village. In the preparations for the 1992 Olympic Games in Atlanta, Georgia, USA, 10,000 people were evicted.

Apartheid has left a terrible legacy of homeless and shelterless people. Government figures estimate that more than seven million people – one quarter of the black population – lack proper housing, 12 million do not have access to safe water and 21 million are without adequate sanitation. Although South Africa is a rich country, the poor living conditions of many of its people mean that the biggest killer of young children is a range of diseases caused by unclean water. Two out of three South Africans now live in urban areas, mainly in the so-called 'black townships'. Others live in 'shacks' in new shanty towns or sleep on the pavements or in the open. People continue to leave impoverished rural areas to find jobs or try to reunite their separated families in the cities. Migrants from other African countries come to South Africa in search of work.

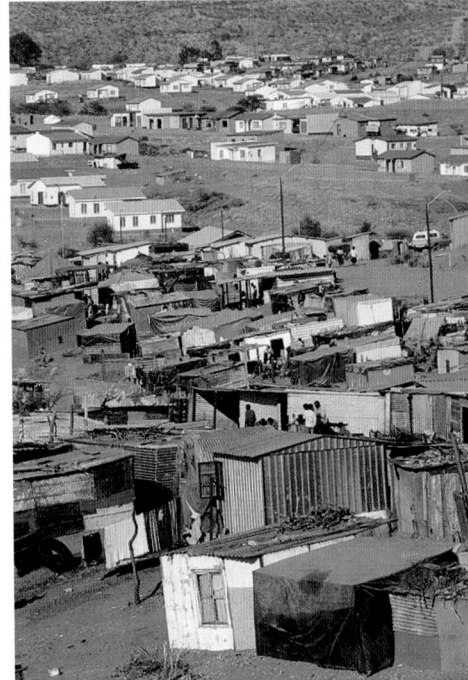

Although the South African government is now building new houses (like those visible in the background), many people will continue to live in poor housing (like the shanty homes in the foreground) for years to come.

Building programmes

When it was elected, the government promised that one million new homes would be built over five years. It said it would give people grants and involve the banks in special house-loan schemes. It would also give direct support to community-based building programmes. But progress has been very slow and the need for new houses continues to grow. Meanwhile many people, like Evelyn, must remain squatters, living on land that does not belong to them. After apartheid ended, Evelyn's family moved back into Cape Town and settled on unused land. Close by their settlement is a wealthy suburb with big homes and lush gardens. But Evelyn's family is again threatened with eviction. More than ever, they feel the injustice of their situation.

Demolishing homes

Over thirty years (1967-97) the Israeli authorities have demolished thousands of Palestinian homes in Israel and the Occupied Territories. Two reasons are given for demolition. First, where a household member is involved in, or suspected of, anti-Israeli activities ('terrorism'). Second, where there is building without permission. Building permits are very difficult to obtain, so many people go ahead and build without one.

When a home is to be demolished, it is surrounded by soldiers and declared a closed military zone. The head of the family is told that he has two hours to remove his furniture and belongings. When the deadline is reached, the family is ordered to move away. Explosives are attached to the house and detonated. The rubble is bulldozed. The family becomes homeless. One of the worst things that a Palestinian can say to anyone is 'Yikhrab baytak' – 'May your house be destroyed'.

These Palestinian children live in an 'unrecognized village'. This means their houses have been built without permission and may be demolished at any time by the Israeli authorities.

The destructiveness of nature

All over the world, people lose their land, their homes and their livelihoods in natural disasters – storms, earthquakes, droughts, floods, landslides and volcanoes. Every country faces a range of natural hazards, although some countries are more vulnerable than others.

Natural disasters cause the greatest destruction in poorer countries. Over 90 per cent of deaths from disasters occur in these countries. Poor people are more likely to live in unsafe housing situated in dangerous areas. They cannot afford to make their homes safe or move to better areas. Even when they try to make improvements, a serious disaster can destroy all their hard work – often in a matter of minutes.

When the rains fail for years in succession, then poor farmers and their families may be forced to leave their homes to seek food aid.

Poor people cannot afford insurance to replace their houses and belongings (even if they could find an insurance company willing to insure their homes in the first place).

Hurricanes can cause massive destruction, especially when buildings are poorly constructed. This is the aftermath of 'Hurricane Joan' in Nicaragua in 1988.

About natural disasters

Some disasters are very large and affect thousands of people, but most are much smaller. Individually these smaller disasters may not kill many people or cause spectacular chaos, but together they inflict tremendous damage. Over five years, around 25,000 natural disasters (floods, earthquakes, landslides, hurricanes etc.) were recorded in Latin America alone; thousands of people were made homeless.

Case study

Vijay lives in the Marathwada region in western India. One night his village was unexpectedly devastated by an earthquake. This is his story:

The night of 30 September 1993, was hot, and Vijay had decided to sleep in the courtyard outside his house to try and keep cool. Suddenly the earth began to shake and the stone walls collapsed around him. An enormous earthquake, measuring 6.3 on the Richter scale, was taking place. Within a few minutes, over 9,500 people were killed, over 30,000 homes were destroyed and a further 200,000 homes were damaged.

At first, the villagers were stunned. Then, desperately, they began to dig in the rubble, hoping to find survivors. They could hear people crying under the stones. Some were rescued, but for most it was too late. Vijay's grandmother and aunt were among those who died.

Hundreds of thousands of people were now homeless. They were also dazed, shocked and confused. Over the years, people had learnt to live with periods of drought and floods, but they knew nothing about earthquakes – Marathwada wasn't in an earthquake zone. But now they were frightened that there would be another earthquake. They didn't want to stay in the village, and they feared returning to their homes.

The government reacted quickly, sending in rescue teams from all parts of India. Tents were provided as temporary shelters, money was sent to buy food and immediate requirements, and medicines helped to prevent the spread of disease. The government said that everyone would be rehoused in better homes. Fifty villages would be rebuilt in a safer location, and people with damaged homes would be offered assistance for repairs.

The Marathwada earthquake of 1993 destroyed over 30,000 homes in western India within a few minutes. Thousands of lives and livelihoods were lost as a result of the tremor.

Months later the rebuilding was still to begin, and a year later only four villages were finished. People spent months living in tents or temporary shelters. Some people were wary of staying inside because they feared another earthquake. Some started to rebuild their homes themselves. Others, whose houses were not so badly damaged, demanded compensation.

Two years after the earthquake struck, Vijay's family was finally rehoused. Their new house was much smaller and flimsier than their old one. It had a corrugated iron roof and got very hot. The old house had been made of local material – stone, mud, timber and thatch – with thick walls to keep out intruders. Even when the temperature rose above 40 degrees outside, the house had been relatively cool inside. It had had a courtyard for sitting and sleeping, a place for animals and for people. Vijay and his family still worry about the future. Even if they are no longer homeless, they do not feel safe.

People in some countries, such as Japan, have learnt to live with earthquakes. The threat is so common that there is a lot of research into predicting and preparing for earthquakes and making buildings safe. Even so, massive damage can still occur.

When an earthquake measuring 7 on the Richter scale hit the Japanese city of Kobe on 17 January, 1995, many of the older buildings collapsed. Over 5,000 people died in the ruins. Thousands more were left homeless in the freezing winter weather. Most went to stay with other family members or were given shelter in schools and community halls. Some people remained living like this for months. Although they were citizens of one of the richest countries in the world, they were homeless.

Shanty towns (*barrios*) built on the hillsides of Latin American cities are in danger of sliding away during heavy rain.

The Kobe earthquake of 1995 destroyed the homes of thousands of city dwellers.

Life in the *barrios*

People who live in crowded conditions in big cities face other risks. In some Latin American cities, poor people live in *barrios* (shanty towns) built on the surrounding hillsides. As more hillsides are cleared and more buildings go up the risks grow. During the rainy season, the land on some of these hillsides begins to slip away, taking the flimsy houses with it.

Caracas, in Venezuela, is one of these cities. It has grown rapidly during the past forty years. In 1950 there were only 700,000 people living there, but by 1990 there were more than three million – three-quarters of them living in the ·barrios. In the 150 years between 1800 and 1950, only twelve landslides had been recorded; but between 1950 and 1970 there were twenty-three. In the 1980s there were an average of twenty landslides each year.

People lose their homes in landslides. Some crowd in with friends and relatives, others are placed in so-called temporary housing – but they can remain there for years. In the end, people have to rely on themselves. Often they begin rebuilding – once again on a hillside which might one day slide away.

Ruined lives

Sudden and unexpected disasters put people under great stress. In 1997, thousands of people became homeless after severe floods in western Poland. A Polish psychiatrist reported that many people were suffering from post-traumatic stress syndrome and that there had been a sudden increase in suicides. Men were less able to cope than women. Some men spent all their compensation money on alcohol. Afterwards, they realised that they had neither home nor compensation – there was nothing left at all.

The misfortunes of war

Talking point

'As people were expelled or murdered, so the destruction of history began. The... bulldozing of mosques, the burning of libraries, the destruction of deeds to... property. In war [the people] leave not a trace of themselves behind.'

Ed Vulliamy, reporter, on the war in Bosnia.

Can you imagine what it would be like to return to your home town to find that nothing of it remained?

People's lives are destroyed by war and conflict. In the past, most of the dead and injured tended to be soldiers. Today, 90 per cent of casualties are ordinary people, mainly women and children. They are the victims of mortar bombs, landmines and aerial bombing. Often the aim of the opposing armies is to kill and injure civilians, rather than each other.

In the same way, people's homes and communities become targets during conflicts. The aim of the warring factions is to damage and destroy homes, shops, places of worship, roads, transport systems, water supplies; to make life so unbearable for people that their only choice is to flee to a safer place or remain homeless amidst the ruins. Those who stay are generally the poorest and weakest people who cannot afford to leave.

Sometimes a whole city faces deliberate destruction. Kabul, the capital of Afghanistan, has been almost razed to the ground by fighting.

The destruction of urban life wrecks people's livelihoods. In Kabul, Afghanistan, a woman collects firewood among the ruins of her city.

The main street in Hargeysa (left), the largest city in north-western Somalia, has been almost entirely destroyed by bombing.

Mogadishu, Somalia's damaged capital, is divided between three groups who run their own separate areas. During the war in former Yugoslavia, Sarajevo and other cities came under constant bombing and sniping. In these situations, it is almost impossible for people to leave. They have to stay – and watch – as their homes and cities are reduced to ruins.

The destruction of a city

This is what happened to Beirut, the capital of Lebanon. Once it was one of the most prosperous and exciting cities in the Middle East, but in 1975 the city became a battleground in a complex and destructive civil war between Lebanon's many different ethnic, religious and political groups. The war continued for fifteen years. By the time a peace accord was signed in 1990, 85,000 people had died in the city alone.

Beirut once had a population of one million people. During the war years, hundreds of thousands of people fled Lebanon. Twenty per cent of the country's population – about 700,000 people – lost their homes. Most of these people lived in Beirut. Many of them lived in the poorest areas in the shanty towns, refugee camps and villages on the southern outskirts.

When their homes were destroyed, people had to live as best they could. Some moved in with relatives but most squatted wherever they found shelter, often in abandoned buildings or underground tunnels. As gunmen took over the city, people sought safety with people of their own political group or religious faith. So they left their homes in mixed areas and went to segregated areas where they felt safer – Christians to the east and north and Muslims to the west and south.

Bosnian Muslim refugees try to create normal life in a refugee camp. They dream of returning to their home towns in Bosnia.

Today the war has ended and Beirut is being rebuilt. All over the city, damaged streets are being cleared and drains and cables are being relaid. New buildings, made from the cheapest materials, are being erected, often without permission. The historic city centre is rising again. Many Lebanese people have returned and business is flourishing. Nevertheless, many people remain homeless, squatting in the ruins. They simply have nowhere else to live.

Case study

Zaynab and her family have been living in the same war-ravaged building in Beirut for more than twelve years....

The building in which Zaynab lives was once an elegant high-rise block. Today it's a ruin. The walls are pock-marked with bullet holes and torn apart by mortar explosions. The windows are boarded-up or covered with plastic. The balconies have collapsed. Zaynab lives in a tiny apartment on the fourth floor with her parents, her sister, three

Even during the worst of the fighting, Zaynab's family remained in Beirut. They feel that they belong to the city and have a future here.

brothers and grandfather. There is no running water, so the women collect it from the taps in the streets below and carry it up the stairs. The building has no proper electricity supply.

Zaynab dreams that one day her family will have a real home. This is not possible at the moment because there are not enough houses and apartments to go round, and those that are available are far too expensive for her family. As squatters, they don't pay rent, although they pay for everything else. Her father and eldest brother are employed, so the family could pay a modest rent. One day someone might want to rebuild on the land and might pay them to move. In the meantime, they will stay here, doing their best to make a difficult and dangerous situation as tolerable as they can. Despite everything, the members of Zaynab's family are glad they have remained in Beirut. They believe that they would have lost everything if they had left. Zaynab's grandfather says: 'I know Palestinians who fled Palestine in 1948.... They thought that they would be coming right back. But they didn't. I vowed that that would never happen to my family.'

Refugees and displaced people

Some of the descendants of the Palestinians mentioned by Zaynab's grandfather also live in Beirut. The refugee camps of Sabra and Chatila in south Beirut look much the same as the surrounding areas, but all the residents are Palestinian refugees. The camps hit the world headlines in September 1982, when 2,000 Palestinians were massacred by Lebanese Christian militias whilst the Israeli army looked on. Three years later, the camps were bombarded by Lebanese Muslim militias.

Despite years of poverty and neglect, Chatila refugee camp remains a home to thousands of Palestinian refugees. Now it is threatened by the construction of a motorway.

Life in Sabra and Chatila remains difficult. People crowd together in tiny huts that they have built themselves. There is no rubbish collection and no sanitation system and the resulting filth seeps through the maze of unpaved alleyways. Some of the heaps of rat-infested rubbish are twenty feet high. There are few facilities, such as health centres or schools, and unemployment is high. The refugees are not allowed to work, and because they are not Lebanese citizens they have no passports and cannot travel.

Today, Sabra and Chatila camps are again under threat. The government intends to demolish them to make way for a new motorway. Those people who can move have already done so. Only the poorest people remain. No one knows where they will go next.

How many refugees?

The United Nations defines a refugee as a person who flees their country because of 'a well founded fear of persecution'. In practice, many refugees flee because of war or conflict. A 'displaced person' is a refugee who stays within the borders of their own country.

United Nations figures from 1997 suggest that, worldwide, there are 23 million refugees and 27 million displaced people. Ninety per cent of these people are in developing countries. Some refugees and displaced people live in camps or hostels, but many more build their own shelters or join earlier refugees. As conflicts end, many people return home – often to find that their houses have been destroyed. Some groups, like the Palestinians, have been refugees for many years, and are likely to remain so for the foreseeable future.

Falling through the safety net

A safety net should break a fall and prevent serious damage. All societies throughout the world have safety nets to support people and prevent them from falling into poverty and isolation. When people become homeless, it is often because their society's safety nets are weakening or have collapsed.

There are many different types of safety net. One kind of safety net might be a personal relationship – like a family, partner or friend, who can help when things go wrong. Our community – our schools, employers, clubs and councils – can be another kind of safety net. Today, we expect government to provide a range of safety nets – social security and pensions and benefits for people who are poor, unemployed, sick, disabled, or who look after others.

In a poor country like Guatemala, family ties are especially important in providing a secure safety net.

A fragile safety net – temporary accommodation in London. Six homeless people share this room.

Support of the family

Families, whether large or small, act as the most common safety net. Close-knit communities in rural areas often help each other and sometimes these links continue when people move to cities. In poorer countries, family and community links are especially important. Where governments are poor, or don't exist at all, they can't provide many benefits. So families and communities are vital in ensuring that people have a place to live.

Families and communities are also important in richer countries, but in these countries we expect the government to act as a safety net. This can mean that the government provides houses for rent or gives people extra income so that they can afford to rent or buy housing. It also means that people are provided with work or training or extra income, so they don't fall into poverty and become homeless.

Temporary housing

In the UK, local councils must provide housing for people with children, pregnant women and people with special needs. Because housing is limited, people may be placed in hostels or 'bed-and-breakfasts' (B&Bs) for long periods. Shelter, an independent housing organization, reported that, in 1996, 76,000 people were placed in B&Bs. Almost 80 per cent of these people were single, and many were refugees, teenagers or mentally-ill people. Temporary housing costs the UK £120 million each year, and the quality is often poor.

Case study

In some countries, the safety nets people used to rely on have collapsed almost completely. Take Tanya, who grew up under the Communist system:

Like other Russians, Tanya believed that the government would always be there to provide a safety net. She had a job and a government flat – neither was great, but she managed. After the Communist system collapsed in the late 1980s, everything went wrong for Tanya. She lost her job and her income, then she was caught passing fake currency notes and was sent to prison. By the time she was released, she had lost her flat and the papers that gave her the right to live in Moscow. So she became homeless, begging on the streets. Her only safety net is a charitable organization which provides free food and medicine. The Russian term for a homeless person is *bomzh*, meaning 'no fixed abode'. The police regard anyone without the proper papers as a *bomzh*. Because Moscow is a prosperous city, many people come to live there without proper papers. The richer people bribe the police, but homeless people cannot afford to pay bribes. Instead they are arrested, beaten, kept in police cells and then dumped outside Moscow. Like Tanya, most find their way back to the city, where the cycle of deprivation starts again.

Since the collapse of Communism, more and more Russians have been forced on to the streets.

Escaping domestic violence

A study carried out in the USA reported that 46 per cent of women in homeless shelters in Chicago were fleeing domestic violence, and 24 per cent were escaping harassment by a former partner.

Almost everywhere, governments are withdrawing the safety nets that were once in place. They say that people should be less dependent on government help. They argue that if people pay less tax, they should have more income to support themselves. They say that if governments no longer build houses and flats for rent, people will have more choice about housing.

However, the result is that it is much harder for poor people to find affordable housing. This is the main reason why people in richer countries are at risk of becoming homeless. There are also other reasons: families are smaller (so there are fewer people to support one another) and divorce and separation are more common. More people live alone. People are less likely to have family or community support when things go wrong.

Some homeless people are disabled. This man from Hong Kong is blind and depends on the charity of passersby.

Case study

Twenty-two-year-old Kerrie, who lives in Margate in southeast England, has fallen through most of society's safety nets:

Kerrie's family life has always been difficult. Her father was an alcoholic. After he'd been drinking he would become violent and beat Kerrie's mum. Finally, Kerrie's mum could stand it no longer – she took the children and left. First, they stayed in a refuge for battered women, then they were given a council house on a big city estate.

For a while, things were okay. Then, when Kerrie was twelve, her mother married again. Kerrie didn't get on with her new stepbrother from the start, but things got much worse when he tried to come into her room at night. At first she fought him off, but he was too strong. She tried to tell her mother, but her mother didn't believe her. So Kerrie left. Not that she got very far. The police soon picked her up for shoplifting some food in a supermarket. She refused to go back home so she was sent to a children's home instead. She ran away from there as well. Each time she ran away, she was sent back. She left for the last time when she turned sixteen.

Since then, Kerrie's life has become even more chaotic. She's stayed in many places, slept on people's floors, shared squats, camped out. Sometimes she's ended up sleeping on the streets. During the summer she worked in a seaside cafe, but in winter everything closed. She was too young to claim social security so she had to beg. By the next summer she was pregnant.

An insecure existence: this mother and her young son live in temporary 'bed-and-breakfast' accommodation in the UK.

When she found that she was pregnant, Kerrie applied for permanent housing but the local council said that there wasn't anything available and, anyway, other people had been waiting for much longer than she had. But, by law, the council had to house pregnant women, so they paid for her to stay in 'bed-and-breakfast' accommodation.

Kerrie says: 'When I came here, I wanted to make a fresh start. But it's been a year and there's still no place for us. I'd like a flat of our own, I could bring my son up properly then. He's got nowhere to play and he keeps getting sick. We've got a roof over our heads, but that's it. At least I get social security now, and child benefit. I get really lonely. Sometimes I just sit and cry.'

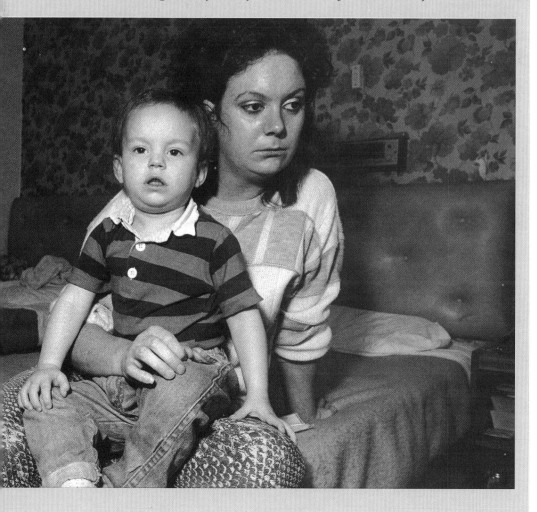

This man once had a secure job and a home. Although he is now homeless, he tries to keep a neat and clean appearance.

Homelessness affects people of all ages, not just the young. Older people may become homeless because of a personal crisis, such as the loss of a job or the death of a partner, or because of a long-standing personal problem, such as an addiction to alcohol or drugs, or mental illness. Their homelessness may be the result of family breakdown, caused by separation, divorce, violence or abuse, or it may be due to factors over which people have no control, such as rising rents and house prices, wars and natural disasters. Whatever the reasons, without the safety nets that family and society can provide, people fall further and faster into homelessness.

Homeless in paradise

'I was homeless and living in Santa Monica, California. A group of us got together to help homeless people get a better chance of getting a job and a place to live. We called our group SHWASHLOCK – SHowers, WASHers and LOCKers. If you're homeless and need a job, you need a place to get clean, have clean clothes and have a place to store your belongings, right?'

Homeless woman, USA.

People who live on the streets for long periods have almost no safety nets. They may lose all contact with their families. Many homeless people have no social security number and receive no government benefits. It can be very hard for them to find regular work. In fact, as far as the government is concerned, they often don't seem to exist.

Health and homelessness

Living on the streets is extremely bad for a person's health. In the UK, so-called 'rough sleepers' live to an average age of only 47, rather than 70 or more. They are much more likely to be murdered or to commit suicide, and they have twenty-five times more chance of contracting tuberculosis than people who have a roof over their heads.

No roof to protect them from the monsoon rain – homeless street children in Bombay huddle under plastic sheets.

Rebuilding a life

Talking point

'Adequate housing is a fundamental human right. Without a right to housing, many other basic human rights are compromised including the right to family life and privacy... the right to health and the right to development.'

Mr Chris Sidoti, Federal Human Rights Commissioner, Australia.

Do you agree with the above statement? How important is housing to the way we live?

As the divide between rich and poor grows wider, more people experience extreme poverty and homelessness.

During the course of this book we have looked at many experiences of homelessness. The reasons why people become homeless, and the ways in which they cope, vary enormously. Despite the great differences, what do these people have in common?

First, people do not choose to become homeless. Like Zaynab in Lebanon and Vijay in India, some people lose their homes suddenly and unexpectedly, or, like Zheng Xiaolong in China, they are forced out to make way for 'development'. However, for most people homelessness is another downward step in a long and unequal fight against poverty, poor health and powerlessness.

Victims of poverty and abuse

Although they might not choose to be homeless, some people prefer life on the street to staying in a violent or abusive family. Juan in Colombia and Kerrie in England left home after

life there became unbearable. Juan still feels the streets have something positive to offer him, Kerrie is desperate to settle in a permanent home.

Second, homeless people are nearly always poor people. The families of Maya in Bombay and Jamilla in Karachi work extremely hard for very low wages. All their earnings go on immediate needs – food, water, clothing, medicines. It is difficult to save money. Yet despite their poverty, many people do manage to improve their shelter or move to a better area. And, as some people move on, more homeless people arrive in the cities.

Campaigning organizations say that there are not enough houses and that the solution is to build more (and better) homes. This is often true. Evelyn is one of

In Mexico City, motorists watch a street child trying to earn money by juggling. All his earnings will go on his immediate needs.

millions of homeless South Africans. Although more houses are being built there, progress is slow. But the situation is often more complex. What if there are enough houses but not of the right size or in the right place or, most importantly, what if they are not available at a price that people can afford? We need to look more critically at how we live and at the inequalities in our societies. Is it right that some people should have large, luxurious houses while others must live in makeshift huts or overcrowded slums or sleep in the streets? Evelyn often asks these questions as she looks from her squatter camp at the huge houses nearby.

The struggle to survive

Third, homeless people are insecure people. Without a home they cannot even begin to plan their future. Every day is a struggle to deal with immediate problems. The first priority must be survival – food for the day, water to drink and to wash with, somewhere to sleep. Longer-term ambitions like getting an education, improving skills or finding a better job seem almost impossible. And taking away basic safety nets, like benefits or access to cheap housing, makes people even more insecure.

Some, but certainly not all, homeless people have personal problems, like addiction to alcohol, hard drugs or gambling. Because they need to satisfy their addictions, they may be pushed into poverty or lose their homes. Similarly, people may lose their homes if they fall ill or have mental health problems. Women may stay in violent relationships rather than risk homelessness. Young people leaving foster care or children's homes may not have the skills to cope with life outside an institution, while ex-prisoners may have difficulty in finding housing. Insecurity means that people lack confidence in themselves and their own abilities. They may lack self-esteem and feel that they are worthless. Like Tanya, they may no longer see themselves as part of society.

The unseen millions

Fourth, homeless people are often invisible people. Mostly, they are unseen and unacknowledged. For example, experts calculate that five million people, many of them homeless, were not included in the 1990 US census. In many countries, if people don't have proper papers they don't exist in law or have any rights. Protest may be difficult or impossible.

Homeless people are demanding action from government to solve the housing crisis. These people are protesting in London.

When we discuss homelessness we are talking about something much broader than a lack of shelter. We are talking about people's right to be treated as human beings. Human rights are at the heart of the debate about homelessness. Yet, in the past, the world's governments and the United Nations have had little to say about it.

Women's building programme

In Kanpur, a city in northern India, half a million people live in 228 slum settlements (areas). Until recently, only 29 of these settlements had adequate toilets and 129 had no toilets at all. Most of the time people go to the toilet where they can. The untreated sewage contaminates water supplies and affects people's health.

Working with the Kanpur Slum Dwellers' Foundation, some Kanpur women met women pavement dwellers from Bombay who had formed groups called Mahila Milan (women's gatherings). Inspired, the Kanpur women formed their own Mahila Milan. Now they are working to improve facilities and learning building skills to construct their own toilets.

In the slums of Addis Ababa, the capital of Ethiopia, women and men work together to build new homes.

57

Today, slowly this is changing. The United Nations Human Rights Commission has a Special Rapporteur on Housing Rights to report on housing and homelessness. United Nations agencies have long been involved in programmes with street children, refugees and victims of disasters. Some governments are finding ways to register homeless people as voters; some are helping them gain access to health services or involving them in planning programmes. These are valuable steps, but they do not in themselves tackle the causes of homelessness.

Organizing for change

Non-government organizations (NGOs) have often been the driving force in supporting homeless people and campaigning for change. There are NGOs all over the world. For example, in the UK there are 2,000 housing NGOs, most of them local NGOs. Without pressure from these groups, politicians and governments would be much less likely to make changes.

Positive support through education and job skills is the first step towards a stable life. These former street children now work in a pizza restaurant in Mwanza, Tanzania.

A hand up, not a hand out, is the aim behind the street paper movement. Here a *Big Issue* vendor shares a joke with a customer.

Homeless people themselves are beginning to organize for change. One initiative is where homeless people sell street papers. Some of the most impressive organizations are found in the poorest countries, like India and South Africa. Often it is homeless women who lead the way. For example, in India homeless women are learning to build neighbourhood facilities.

Homeless people are now forming international organizations to lobby for better and more secure housing and to learn from each other. One such organization is the International Federation of the Homeless Poor (also called the International Slum Dwellers' Network). So far, it has member organizations in India, Sri Lanka, Thailand, Cambodia, the Philippines, Namibia and South Africa. Together they show that the fight against homelessness is also a fight against poverty and inequality and in favour of human rights for all.

Street papers

In 1989 the world's first street paper was launched in New York. *Street News* was sold by homeless people who bought copies and resold them at a fixed price. This way they earned a small income while gaining skills and confidence. One year later, the *Big Issue* was launched in the UK.

Today, there are almost 100 street papers worldwide – around 40 in the USA and Canada, 60 in western Europe and others in Australia, Russia and South Africa. Germany, Europe's richest country, has 35 street papers. The papers sell widely and, as well as helping homeless people, they keep the issue of homelessness in the public eye. All the papers look and read very differently, but their aim is the same: 'a hand up, not a hand out'.

Glossary

Addiction Total dependence (for example, on alcohol or drugs).

Bed-and-breakfast Temporary housing (in the UK). Residents often have to be out of their bed-and-breakfast accommodation by 10am and so spend their days on the streets.

Bombay India's largest city, with over 12 million people, now officially renamed Mumbai.

Charitable organization An organization which aims to help people or to provide something without making a profit.

Communist system A system in which the government owns and runs most businesses.

Depression A situation in which the economy slows down and unemployment rises.

Drop-in centre A location which provides services that people can use without having to make a prior appointment.

Environmental degradation The poisoning of land, water and air, or land erosion.

Eviction The order (by the authorities, or by a private landlord) to leave an area or building.

Global warming Climate change worldwide (caused by environmental degradation).

Homeless shelter Temporary (often overnight) bed and facilities (often run by charities).

Initiative A new way of doing things.

Militia A group of fighters (usually linked to a political group).

Palestinians The Arabic-speaking people of Palestine in the Middle East, many of whom fled their homes as refugees in 1948 after their land was claimed by Israel as a homeland for Jewish people. Many Palestinians stayed in refugee camps in other Arab countries, such as Jordan or Lebanon, or in areas later occupied by Israel (called Palestinian Occupied Territories).

Pension A payment, often by government, to a retired or disabled person.

Rapporteur A person who investigates an issue on behalf of an agency, and reports back.

Refugee A person who flees their country to escape persecution.

Richter scale A scale which measures (from 1 to 10) the strength of an earthquake (the greater the strength of the earthquake, the higher the number).

Rough sleeper A person who sleeps in the open (usually in the street).

Segregate To separate.

Sharecropper A farm-worker or tenant who shares the crop with the owner of the land.

Slum A run-down, overcrowded building (the term is often used to describe an area or neighbourhood).

Social security Government benefit payment.

Squat The occupation (by squatters) of an empty or unused building or land without the consent of the owner.

Squatter camp A settlement of makeshift homes constructed on empty, unused or waste land, often against the law.

Tuberculosis An infectious disease affecting people's lungs, mainly found in poorer countries.

Urban Town or city life.

Books to Read

Academic

An Urbanizing World: Global Report on Human Settlements 1996, Oxford University Press, 1996. The most comprehensive world survey of housing and homelessness. Available from the United Nations Centre for Human Settlements (HABITAT).

Environment and Urbanization A twice-yearly journal on housing and homelessness in the developing world. Available from the International Institute for Environment and Development, 3 Endsleigh Street, London WC1H 0DD, UK.

Poverty and Health: Reaping a Richer Harvest by Marie-Thérèse Feuerstein, Macmillan, 1997. Written for development workers, but a useful resource for teachers and students exploring links in poverty and development.

For schools and teachers

'Accommodating Differences' Schools Resources Pack Looks at housing issues in India, South Africa and Belfast, Northern Ireland, through case studies, activities and illustrations. It has an excellent resource section. Available from Homeless International, Guildford House, 20 Queen's Road, Coventry CV1 3EG, UK.

Doorways by Barbara Taylor, Save the Children, 1992. Examines global housing issues through activities, case studies and photos. Case studies include Argentina, Bangladesh, India, Sudan, UK. Available from BEBC Distribution, PO Box 1496, Parkstone, Poole, Dorset BH12 3YD, UK.

Fala Favala Life in a *favala* (shanty town) in San Paolo, Brazil, with case studies and illustrations. CAFOD, 1992. Available from BEBC Distribution, as above.

Human Rights - Shelter by Kate Haycock, Wayland, 1993. How people seek shelter around the world and some of the problems they encounter.

In the Shadow of the City by Sue Greig, Anne Shrosbree and Bill Hamblett, Save the Children, 1991. A teaching pack looking at city life, with case studies from South America and UK.

One Person's Ceiling by Theresa MacDermott and Julie Swallow, Shelter, 1998. A teacher's guide to housing, homelessness and young people in the UK.

A Right to a Roof Four handbooks on homes, sustainable development, homelessness and conflict. Case studies include Colombia, Costa Rica, India, Israel and Palestine, Somalia, Sri Lanka, Uganda and UK. Council for Education in World Citizenship, 1994. Available from CEWC, 15 St Swithin's Lane, London EC4N 8AL, UK.

Who are the Street Children? Examines the background and situation of street children in Brazil, including individual case studies. The pack consists of 28 colour slides, 10 black-and-white photos, and a book for teachers. Available from UNICEF UK, Unit 1, Rignals Lane, Chelmsford, Essex CM2 8TU, UK.

Useful Addresses

Magazines and newsletters

New Internationalist Monthly magazine; especially issues 276 (February 1996) *Housing and Homelessness* and 283 (September 1996) *Field of Dreams: Life in a Refugee Settlement*. Available from NI, 55 Rectory Road, Oxford OX4 1BW, UK.

Local street papers (*Big Issue*, etc)

Fiction

Kiss the Dust by Elizabeth Laird, Mammoth, 1991. A refugee Kurdish girl flees her homeland in Iraq.

No Roof in Bosnia by Els de Groen, Spindlewood, 1997. Four children from different ethnic backgrounds in Bosnia band together to escape persecution.

Throwaways by Ian Strachan, Mammoth, 1992. In a fictional future, abandoned children are forced to live as pickers on the city rubbish tip.

The Tortilla Curtain by T Coraghessan Boyle, Bloomsbury, 1995.
The contrasting lives of rich Californians and poor Mexican immigrants.

Worldwide, there are many thousands of organizations working to end homelessness at international, national or local levels.

Europe/International

European Federation of National Organizations Working with the Homeless (FEANTSA)
1 Rue Defacqz 1000
Brussels, Belgium
E-mail:feantsa@compuserve.com

United Nations Centre for Human Settlements (HABITAT)
Europe Office
Room E-6.1
Palais des Nations
1211 Geneva 10, Switzerland

UK

Homeless International
Guildford House
20 Queens Road
Coventry CV1 3EG, UK
E-mail: rm@homeint.win-uk.net

Shelter
88 Old Street
London EC1V 9HU, UK
http://www.shelter.org.uk

Shelter Cymru
25 Walter Road
Swansea SA1 1ZZ, UK

Shelter (Northern Ireland)
165 University Street
Belfast BT17 1HR, UK

Shelter (Scotland)
8 Hamilton Terrace
Edinburgh EH12 5JD, UK

Y Care International
640 Forest Road
London E17 3DZ, UK
E-mail: ycareint@compuserve.com
Website: http://www.oneworld.org/ymcacare

USA

National Coalition for the Homeless
1612 K Street NW, no 1004
Washington DC 2006, USA

Index

Numbers in **bold** refer to illustrations.